DATE DUE

MAR 1 3 2008			
MAR 2 6 2008			
FEB 11 2011			

MONSTERS

KING KONG

By Adam Woog

KIDHAVEN PRESS

An imprint of Thomson Gale, a part of The Thomson Corporation

THOMSON

™

GALE

Detroit • New York • San Francisco • New Haven, Conn. • Waterville, Maine • London

For Karen Kent, the other KK in my life.

© 2007 Thomson Gale, a part of The Thomson Corporation.

Thomson and Star Logo are trademarks and Gale and KidHaven Press are registered trademarks used herein under license.

For more information, contact
KidHaven Press
27500 Drake Rd.
Farmington Hills, MI 48331-3535
Or you can visit our Internet site at http://www.gale.com

LIBRARY OF CONGRESS CATALOGING-IN-PUBLICATION DATA

Woog, Adam, 1953–
King Kong / by Adam Woog.
    p. cm. — (Monsters)
  Includes bibliographical references and index.
ISBN 13: 978-0-7377-3585-7
ISBN 10: 0-7377-3585-6 (hard cover : alk. paper)
  1. King Kong (Motion picture : 1933)—Juvenile literature. 2. King Kong (Motion picture : 2005)—Juvenile literature. I. Title. II. Series.
PN1997.K437W66 2006
791.43'72—dc22
                                                   2006012327

Printed in the United States

CONTENTS

CHAPTER 1

THE BIGGEST GORILLA

King Kong is a giant gorilla and a movie star. Since his first appearance more than 70 years ago, he has become one of the most famous movie monsters in the world. In fact, to his fans, the big ape is the greatest movie monster ever.

He has appeared in many films, but the best-known two are both called *King Kong*. The first is a classic black-and-white movie from 1933. The other is a three-hour epic from 2005.

These two versions differ in some ways, but they tell the same basic story. It is a version of the old tale of Beauty and the Beast, about a friendship between two mismatched characters. In *King Kong*, the Beast's tender love for Beauty leads to tragedy.

A Desperate Filmmaker

In the 2005 movie, the story opens in 1933, when the United States is enduring the Great Depression. Millions of people are unemployed, starving, and miserable. **Breadlines** and other signs of desperate times are common sights.

In New York City, Carl Denham, a director of adventure **documentaries**, needs to raise money for his latest project. But Carl is unpredictable and reckless. He is not popular with the heads of the movie studio. In fact, they plan to cancel his project.

King Kong is considered by some to be the cinema's greatest monster.

Desperate, Carl steals the part of the film that he has already made. He hires a ship to take him to a remote island in the South Seas. He persuades an actress, Ann Darrow, to join his project. He also tricks a writer, Jack Driscoll, into coming so he can finish the movie's **screenplay**.

Carl gathers the rest of his film crew and sailors just in time. They sail away right before the police come to arrest the filmmaker. A mysterious, exciting, and possibly dangerous sea voyage awaits them.

KIDNAPPED!

The film crew's destination is Skull Island, a remote spot in the South Pacific. It is surrounded by fog, so no outsiders know about it. According to legend, it is ruled by Kong, an ape that is 50 feet (15.24m) tall.

In a scene from the 2005 movie, Ann looks on in horror as she waits to be sacrificed to Kong.

When the ship gets to Skull Island, a fierce storm runs it aground. While the sailors repair the ship, Carl, Ann, Jack, and the film crew go ashore. A group of terrifying natives attacks them there. Some members of the film crew are killed, but the sailors arrive in time to save most of them.

The survivors go back to the ship, but before they can escape the island, a native sneaks aboard and kidnaps Ann. The natives worship Kong and want to please him by **sacrificing** Ann to him. They tie her up near a huge wall separating their settlement from the rest of the island.

Taken by Kong

When the men on the ship realize that Ann is gone, they rush to rescue her. Leading them is Jack, who has fallen in love with Ann. But the men are too late. Kong gets to Ann first and takes her deep into the jungle.

The ship's captain stays behind, but Carl and Jack go after Ann. They take several sailors and the film crew. Along the way, they see many other strange animals—prehistoric creatures, such as dinosaurs, that have survived for millions of years in isolation. And the men have many close calls. For example, they are nearly killed in a brontosaurus stampede.

Meanwhile, Ann is Kong's captive. She has not been killed as earlier sacrifices had been. But she is still in danger, so the actress protects herself by

Kong and Ann bonded after he captured her.

dancing, juggling, and otherwise entertaining Kong. The big ape is fascinated by Ann and protects her from the other creatures. In return, Ann becomes fond of Kong.

ESCAPE FROM KONG

When Kong spots Ann's rescue party approaching, he attacks them. Many of the men fall down a ravine, where they fight giant worms and other creatures. Some die, but the ship's captain arrives and saves the others.

King Kong

Ann, in the meantime, has realized that Kong can protect her in the fierce jungle. She becomes less afraid and lets the big gorilla carry her around. At Kong's mountaintop home, they peacefully watch a beautiful sunset together.

Jack continues searching for Ann on his own. When he finds her, the two escape down a cliff. Kong chases them, but Carl and the surviving crew members are waiting for him on the shore with a trap.

Kong bravely protects Ann from a charging dinosaur on Skull Island.

This is because Carl has a new idea. He wants to capture Kong and bring him back to New York City. The filmmaker knows that people will pay a fortune to see such an amazing creature.

Ann begs Carl not to carry out the plan. She does not want Kong to be injured or kept in chains far from his home. But Carl succeeds in conquering Kong, and the ship takes him to New York City.

BACK IN NEW YORK

In New York, Carl shows a chained Kong to the public, advertising him as the Eighth Wonder of the World. He plans to re-create on stage Ann's capture by the giant monster. An excited audience gathers to witness this spectacle.

However, the blonde actress in Carl's show is not Ann. Ann has refused to be part of the show because she cannot stand to see Kong treated cruelly. Instead, she has a low-paying job as a dancer in another show. Jack is also not there. He is sadly watching a comedy that he wrote for Ann. He thinks she should have been its star.

When Kong realizes that the the actress is not Ann, he is furious. The big ape is also confused by the crowds and the flashes from cameras. In a mighty rage, he breaks free and runs into the streets of the city, desperately searching for Ann. Jack spots Kong and leads him away from the city's crowded areas. Kong hates Jack because he helped take Ann away, so the giant gorilla chases after him.

BEAUTY KILLS THE BEAST

When Ann hears that Kong has escaped, she finds him and calms him down. He carries her to Central Park, where they slide around on a frozen lake. But this moment of happiness is interrupted when army soldiers attack Kong.

Kong escapes by climbing New York's most famous skyscraper, the Empire State Building. He gently holds Ann in one hand while he climbs. The

Kong and Ann share a tender moment as he gently holds her at the top of the Empire State Building.

two pause to watch a beautiful sunset, just as they did in the jungle. But their peaceful moment is interrupted by attacking military **biplanes**.

Ann wants to stay with Kong, but he sets her down and climbs to the top of the building. Ann tries to attract the attention of the planes' pilots, hoping to stop them, but she cannot. Kong destroys several planes but is badly injured and falls to his death.

A curious crowd gathers around the body of Kong on the street below. Jack tries to comfort Ann, who is grief stricken. The movie ends as Carl Denham says, "It wasn't the airplanes. It was beauty killed the beast."[1]

Old and New

That famous line is used in both the 2005 version of *King Kong* and the original 1933 film. The first movie remains a classic. It pioneered many techniques in movie special effects, and its powerful story can still thrill audiences. To his fans, it does not matter that the 1933 Kong was really only eighteen inches (45.72cm) tall!

Chapter 2

The Original Kong

Two Americans, Ernest B. Schoedsack and Merian C. Cooper, created the original *King Kong*. They were brave daredevil filmmakers just like the character Carl Denham. During World War I (1914–18), both had exciting adventures. Cooper, a pilot, was badly injured and spent time in a German camp for prisoners of war. Schoedsack was a newsreel cameraman who loved going to dangerous war zones.

After the war, the adventurers teamed up to make movies, specializing in thrilling documentaries. They traveled the world to find wild animals and unusual people. Their motto was "Keep It Distant, Difficult, and Dangerous."[2]

13

WRITING KING KONG

The two filmmakers were successful, but they wanted to create fiction movies as well as documentaries. In 1931, Cooper started working on a story called *The Beast*. It was about a gorilla that was tamed and brought to civilization.

Cooper persuaded a movie studio, RKO, to give him money to finish the story. A famous thriller writer named Edgar Wallace was hired to help him. Wallace contributed many good ideas, but fell ill and died in 1932.

Ernest Schoedsack and Fay Wray look at a promotional poster for 1933's King Kong.

Two other writers joined Cooper: James A. Creelman and Ruth Rose, who was Schoedsack's wife. As they refined the story, its title changed from *The Beast* to *The Eighth Wonder*, then to *Kong*, and finally to *King Kong*. Its main character also changed greatly as the normal-sized gorilla became a 50-foot (15.24m) monster.

The writers invented many parts of the story. For example, there are no giant gorillas in real life. Furthermore, real gorillas are usually peaceful vegetarians, not fierce killers. On the other hand, not everything in *King Kong* was made up. For example, the scenes showing poverty in the United States were realistic for that era. The writers knew that audiences would understand what a breadline was and why Ann was so hungry that she tried to steal an apple.

THE ACTORS

As the screenplay took shape, Schoedsack and Cooper hired actors. The part of Carl Denham was given to Robert Armstrong, who modeled his headstrong daredevil character on Cooper himself. Jack Driscoll, the ship's first mate in this version, was played by the inexperienced but handsome Bruce Cabot.

The role of Ann Darrow went to the beautiful young actress Fay Wray. Cooper told Wray that her costar would be "the tallest, darkest leading man in Hollywood."[3] She thought he meant one of the era's major stars, Cary Grant.

Kong viciously fights off a pterodactyl that is trying to capture Ann in this scene from the 1933 movie.

Meanwhile, Cooper and Schoedsack needed to cast the most important role—Kong. They knew they would have to use special effects. This field was in its infancy in 1933. Nonetheless, the filmmakers realized that it could bring their giant gorilla to life.

STOP-MOTION ANIMATION

Cooper and Schoedsack hired a brilliant special effects artist, Willis O'Brien, to create Kong using

stop-motion animation. Using this technique, small models are filmed just one shot, or **frame**, at a time. In between, the models are moved very slightly. Then, when the film runs at normal speed, the models seem to move by themselves.

Stop-motion works because movie frames are really still photos, shown quickly one after the other. Movie film usually runs at 24 frames per second, so fast that it creates the illusion of smooth motion.

The technique seems simple now, but in 1933 it was amazing and delightful. It was slow work, though. The filmmakers had to move the models 24 times to make just one second of film!

BUILDING KONG

To create a stop-motion Kong, O'Brien and his chief assistant, Marcel Delgado, first built an aluminum skeleton. It was only 18 inches (45.72cm) high. The skeleton had joints, so its arms and legs could be moved.

Over this tiny model went a body of cotton and foam rubber, with a covering of latex and rabbit fur. O'Brien's team also made glass eyeballs and movable eyebrows, lips, and nose. Wires through the model's skull controlled these features.

An extra Kong was needed as well because the rubber skin dried out under the hot studio lights and had to be replaced regularly. This took time, so having a second Kong meant filming could go faster. But because the skin on Kong's head was

An eighteen-inch model of Kong (pictured) was used to create stop-motion animation for the 1933 film.

replaced frequently, his face changes a little throughout the movie.

Furthermore, viewers can often see Kong's fur move because the crew's fingers moved it around between shots. At first the filmmakers were unhappy about this. Then they realized that it made it seem like Kong's fur was rippling because of a breeze—or because he was mad!

MORE SPECIAL EFFECTS

Several big Kong models were made for close-ups. For example, head-and-shoulders were made of

wood, cloth, rubber, and bearskin, with 12-inch (30.48cm) eyeballs and 10-inch (25.4cm) fangs. Three crewmembers sat inside this to move its features. Two big hands were also needed: One to appear in the cave scene and another with movable fingers to hold Wray.

Skull Island's other creatures were also miniatures, 18 inches (45.72cm) to 3 feet (.91m) long. O'Brien's crew built other miniature props such as ships, subway trains, and fighter planes. They also

Though made from wood, rubber, and rabbit fur, a Kong model looks amazingly lifelike.

built sets, tiny stages that held these props. The sets made Kong look about 25 feet (7.62m) tall. This size was chosen as a better size than Cooper's original 50-foot (15.24m) monster.

Besides these, many other special-effects techniques were used. For example, in some scenes, rear projection showed film of animals on a screen behind the actors. This created the illusion that the creatures and humans were in the same place.

SOUND

These visuals were enhanced by the use of sound. Sound was still an exciting new development in movies. The first sound film, or "talkie," had appeared only a few years before in 1927. Part of *King Kong*'s excellent sound was its dramatic musical score by composer Max Steiner.

But the movie used sound-effects on a much larger scale than ever before. The imaginative plot forced the sound effects crew to invent many new techniques. For example, sound editor Murray Spivack created Kong's famous roar by combining the roar of a lion and a tiger, then running it backwards at low speed.

Spivack made the sound of Kong's footsteps by wrapping toilet plungers in foam rubber and stomping them in a box filled with gravel. And the noise of Kong beating his chest was Spivack hitting his assistant on the chest with a padded drumstick. But one sound was real—Wray did her own screaming!

A poster advertises the eagerly awaited 1933 release of King Kong.

The movie's complicated sound and special effects meant that progress was slow. Creating *King Kong* took about a year, much longer than average. And it cost about $670,000, well over twice as much as an average RKO movie in those days.

The studio's executives were worried about the time and money. When they saw the finished product, however, they realized they had a hit. RKO enthusiastically approved a big advertising campaign that called *King Kong* "the picture destined to startle the world."[4]

KONG RELEASED

It was, indeed, an amazing success. In fact, it was the blockbuster of its time. When *King Kong* opened in 1933, critics raved and crowds stood in theater lines that stretched around the block. The movie smashed all previous **box office** records–no one had ever seen anything like it.

Nonetheless, the film was not nominated for even one Academy Award. If there had been an award for special effects it would surely have won, but there was no such category at the time.

King Kong's success inspired a sequel and many imitations. The biggest and best of these was released in 2005. In that movie, director Peter Jackson showed how much the world of special effects has changed since 1933.

King Kong

CHAPTER 3

THE RETURN OF KONG

Peter Jackson, the mastermind behind the 2005 King Kong remake, is a gifted director from New Zealand. He is best known for another epic: the *Lord of the Rings* **trilogy**. But making *King Kong* was the dream of a lifetime for Jackson because the 1933 classic has always been his favorite film.

Jackson first saw the movie on television when he was nine years old, growing up in the small town of Pukerua Bay. It had such a powerful impact that he immediately decided to become a filmmaker. He says, "I can't tell you what an effect it had on me. [*King Kong*] put me on the path to where I am today."[5]

Soon after, Jackson's parents gave him a small movie camera, and he began making films. One was a version of *King Kong*. He built his own sets and used pieces of his mother's old fur **stole** to make a tiny Kong.

OLD STORY, NEW AUDIENCE

When Jackson grew up and became a successful director, he knew that many young people did not know about the black-and-white *King Kong*. He

Peter Jackson, a longtime King Kong *fan, directed the 2005 version of the movie.*

dreamed of making his own version. The director wanted to share the story he loved so much.

In 1996, Jackson wrote a screenplay about the giant ape. It was quite different from the original. It had lots of comedy along with plenty of adventure.

Universal Studios turned down Jackson's screenplay. Several other remakes of classic monster movies, including *Godzilla*, had recently done poorly. So Jackson began another project: *The Lord of the Rings*.

Its smash success established Jackson as one of the best known and most powerful directors in the world. Afterward, he could make any movie he wanted. He chose *King Kong*.

A NEW VERSION

Jackson started by completely rewriting his screenplay. He worked with two other New Zealand writers —his wife, Fran Walsh, and Philippa Buyers. The three had worked together before on the *Lord of the Rings* screenplay.

The new *King Kong* was in some ways close to the 1933 original, but there were some changes. For example, the poverty of the Depression years had to be stressed for modern audiences. Also, Jack Driscoll's character was changed from first mate to screenwriter.

The biggest changes included giving the characters more complicated emotions. For example, in the original, Jack is not very smart or sensitive. The

The character of Carl, played by Jack Black, changes from likeable to cold and heartless.

2005 version makes him more realistic. Also, the original Carl is likeable throughout the story. In the new version, he turns cold and heartless after deciding to capture Kong.

Furthermore, in the original the gorilla is merely a fierce killer. In the remake, he has more complex emotions, including love for Ann. Also, in the earlier movie, Ann feels only fear toward the ape. In the new version, she conquers her fear and tries to protect him.

 King Kong

ACTORS

As the screenplay took shape, Jackson worked on other aspects of the movie. This included selecting performers for its key roles. A beautiful British actress, Naomi Watts, was chosen to play Ann Darrow. Tall, soulful-eyed Adrien Brody filled the role of Jack Driscoll. The part of Carl Denham went to comic actor Jack Black. Jackson also gave himself a small role. In the biplane scene, he appears briefly as a pilot—the same **cameo** Cooper and Schoedsack had in the original.

The director had hoped that Fay Wray, the original Ann Darrow, would play an elderly lady who

Andy Serkis (second from left) and Naomi Watts (center) take direction from Peter Jackson (right) during the filming of King Kong.

comes from the crowd to speak the movie's last line about beauty killing the beast. Unfortunately, Wray passed away before the scene was shot, so Carl Denham, as in the original, had the line.

Another key actor was Andy Serkis, a talented British performer. Although Serkis had a small role as Lumpy, the cook, he also had a much longer–although invisible–part. Thanks to magical special effects, he portrayed the most realistic Kong ever filmed.

Serkis prepared for his role by studying gorillas carefully. He watched hundreds of hours of videos, then observed the apes at the London Zoo and in the wild, in the African nation of Rwanda.

CREATING KONG

After Serkis learned how to imitate a gorilla, Jackson and his team filmed him using a technique called motion capture. This is the same technique Jackson used to turn Serkis into Gollum in *Lord of the Rings*. In motion capture, or mocap, dozens of small, mirrored spots are attached to an actor. In this case, the mirrors were on a bulky blue gorilla suit.

Cameras recorded Serkis's movements as he acted in front of a blue screen. Technicians later removed everything from the footage except the mirrored spots. What was left was a three-dimensional map of Serkis's movements. Animators then used this to create Kong using computer-generated imagery (CGI). Dozens of artists were needed to make

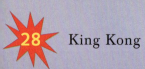

sure that even the tiniest details, such as Kong's fur waving in the breeze, looked perfect.

OTHER SPECIAL EFFECTS

Jackson filled his movie with many other special effects. In fact, the movie's 2,400 special-effects shots set a new record. Like most of the live action in the movie, they were created at Wata Workshop, Jackson's studio in New Zealand.

Many moments in *King Kong* combined several techniques, such as live action, CGI, and miniature sets, all at once. For example, the brontosaurus

Special-effects computers helped create realistic dinosaurs and other fantasic beasts.

stampede scene began with actors on treadmills pretending to run away. These images were combined with film that used miniature sets and computer-generated creatures.

The brontosauruses in this scene were based on dinosaurs that once existed, but many of Skull Island's other creatures were pure fantasy. Jackson and his team simply imagined what millions of years of isolated **evolution** might have created. This resulted in such monsters as the foetadon, which chases Ann into a log and is then eaten by another imaginary creature, *Vastatasaurus rex.*

Jackson also combined live action with special effects to re-create New York City's busy streets. In reality, the set was only one story high and about four blocks square. But Jackson's team added thousands of computer-generated buildings and people to make it seem like a big city.

KONG RELEASED AGAIN!

In every instance, Jackson's team worked hard to make their imaginary world as realistic as possible. As one of Jackson's coworkers remarked, "Big credit to the actors and to Peter to shoot something that has so little reality in it, and then suddenly it ends up looking amazing."[6] This painstaking attention to detail meant that the movie took a long time to shoot. It was also very expensive. Its final cost, about $207 million, was one of the biggest budgets ever for a film.

Peter Jackson directs Naomi Watts as the crew waits to film the upcoming scene.

While he was shooting, Jackson regularly posted production diary entries on the Internet. These gave fans early, behind-the-scenes glimpses of his project. The online entries went against the usual policy of Hollywood movie studios, which normally close their sets and keep things secret.

The diaries whetted the fans' appetites, who eagerly looked forward to *King Kong*. The movie was a huge hit when it was released in December 2005. It won three Academy Awards, and many critics named it one of the top movies of the year.

Jackson's *King Kong* renewed public interest in the big creature, and he is more popular than ever. In fact, though, he has never gone away. Since 1933, Kong has been a constant presence around the world.

CHAPTER 4

KONG IN THE WORLD

When it was first made in the 1930s, no one suspected that *King Kong* would become such a hit. Nor could anyone have foreseen that it would be so popular for so many decades, or that it would inspire so many imitations. But it did, and the mighty ape has long since entered the public mind as one of the most famous movie monsters of all time. Almost everyone knows who Kong is.

The original movie has long been a classic, recognized as a brilliant pioneer in combining special effects with a thrilling story line. In 1975, the American Film Institute declared that it was one of the fifty best American films ever made. It is often named in other lists of the greatest films of all time.

MOVIE IMITATIONS

The immediate popularity of *King Kong* inspired a sequel right away. *Son of Kong*, made by the same directors, is about a return trip to Skull Island and the discovery of Kong's son. It was followed over the next decades by many more movies—some good, some bad—that featured giant apes. Among these are *Konga, King Kong Escapes, King of Kong Island, Queen Kong, King Kong Lives*, and two versions of *Mighty Joe Young*.

Furthermore, the success of *King Kong* inspired a fad for monster movies starring other giant beasts.

King Kong vs. Godzilla *was one of many films inspired by the first* King Kong *movie.*

Among these were *Attack of the 50-Foot Woman* and *Godzilla*. Godzilla and King Kong even met in a movie called *King Kong vs. Godzilla*. In this movie, Kong is at least five times as big as in the original, and he can shoot electricity from his fingers!

Still another movie version of the story was released in 1976. Also called *King Kong*, it starred two fine actors, Jessica Lange and Jeff Bridges. It updated the setting to 1976, so that in the last scene the giant ape climbs one of the twin towers of the World Trade Center in New York City.

But this movie was very different from the original. Its plot was meant to make a statement about the environment, but it seemed more like a lecture than an exciting story. Also, an actor in a gorilla suit played Kong, and he was not very convincing. This version was not popular with either critics or audiences.

OTHER MOVIE STUFF

Several movies that are not exactly about Kong have made references to the giant ape. For example, scenes from *King Kong* are imitated in all three *Jurassic Park* films. Kong is even mentioned directly in the first one. As the tour group approaches the huge Jurassic Park gate, the character Dr. Ian Malcolm jokes, "What've they got in there, King Kong?"[7]

Several animated movies have also made reference to the famous ape. For instance, in one scene of *Chicken Little*, the character Fish imitates the Em-

King Kong

Gromit flies past the angry were-rabbit in a scene similar to the one made famous by the original King Kong *film.*

pire State Building scene, and the famous "beauty killed the beast" line is quoted.

In *Wallace & Gromit: The Curse of the Were-Rabbit*, the giant were-rabbit imitates Kong by beating its chest and taking Lady Tottington captive and up onto a tall building. It is appropriate that a Wallace & Gromit movie honors *King Kong* in this way. The technique that is used to make the Wallace & Gromit films is Claymation—a more sophisticated version of the stop-motion photography that Willis O'Brien pioneered in the 1933 classic.

TV

Many television shows have also starred or been inspired by the big ape. These include a cartoon series called *The King Kong Show* as well as episodes of *Duck Tales, Tiny Toon Adventures, Garfield and Friends,* and *The Simpsons.* The *Simpsons* episode starred Homer as Kong, Marge as Ann, and Mr. Burns as Carl Denham. In it, "King Homer" collapses in exhaustion after failing to climb beyond the first story of a tall building.

The character of Kong has also appeared in several commercials. One advertised Energizer batteries. It featured a rival company hiring Kong to kill the Energizer Bunny—unsuccessfully, of course. Another popular commercial, for the Volkswagen Touareg, gave viewers a glimpse backstage of Jackson's film in the making.

There are even two television stations named in the big ape's honor! KING is a longtime TV station in Seattle. When the company launched a sister station, executives naturally decided that it should be called KONG.

COLLECTIBLES

The giant gorilla has also found his way into many other places. When *King Kong* was released in 1933, it benefited from a huge advertising campaign. The country—and in time the whole world—was flooded with promotional material about the movie. This

This movie poster (right) from the 1933 King Kong *is just one of many items sought by collectors.*

material is very rare and valuable today. For instance, an original poster in good condition can sell for tens of thousands of dollars. Especially valuable are programs from the movie's gala Hollywood premiere. These were lavish 28-page brochures, with covers made from real copper!

The 1976 version of *King Kong* also had a massive ad campaign. Dozens of different kinds of **memorabilia** and **collectibles** were produced. These included thermoses, wallpaper, dolls, balloons, and games. Other items were clocks, posters, binders, and Halloween costumes, along with keychains, lunch boxes, jigsaw puzzles, and stickers. More recently, Jackson's version of the movie has inspired a similar blizzard of stuff.

Unconnected to specific movies, manufacturers over the years have also produced everything from Kong-shaped salt-and-pepper shakers and stuffed toys to Kong-shaped soap and chocolate. Of course, at the Empire State Building, many Kong-related items are for sale in the gift shop. Many of these things can also be found in specialty stores or online auction sites.

Books and Comics

A number of books have been produced about Kong over the years. The earliest of these was connected to the original 1933 films. It was a novel that told the story of the movie, and it actually came out just before the movie's release.

In the decades since, there have been dozens of others. These range from serious nonfiction books by film scholars to lighthearted fictional spoofs such as *My Side by King Kong.* This was a fake autobiography that claimed that the natives of Skull Island were actually a shipwrecked musical-theater touring company!

Comic book artists have also often been inspired by the story of Kong. One example was a graphic novel published in 2005 by Dark Horse Comics.

Fay Wray, pictured here in Kong's giant hand, titled her autobiography On the Other Hand.

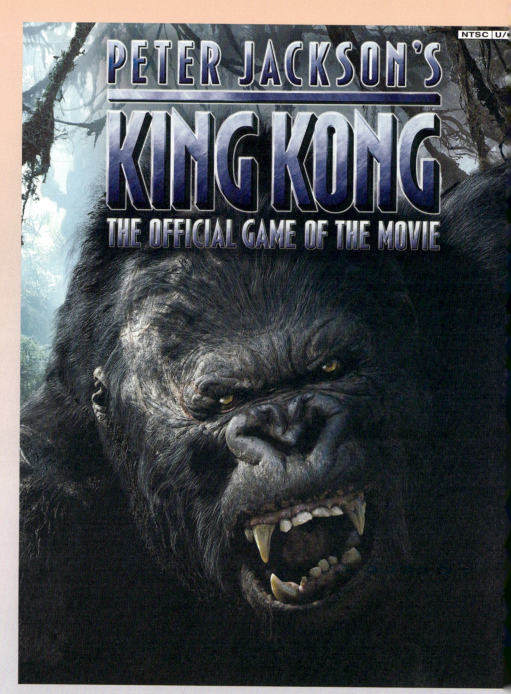

NTSC U/

A *King Kong* video game was released after the 2005 movie came out.

And Fay Wray, the original Ann Darrow, titled her autobiography *On the Other Hand* in honor of the famous scenes of Kong holding her in his massive hand.

OTHER STUFF

The mighty ape has popped up in many other places as well. In 1983, for example, a 40-foot (12.19m) balloon of Kong was placed on top of the Empire State Building to celebrate the original film's fiftieth anniversary. And for decades the Universal Studios theme parks in California and Florida have featured major attractions starring Kong.

Kong has also played a big role in video games. For example, in the 1980s he was the inspiration for a now-classic game, *Donkey Kong*. More recently, *Peter Jackson's King Kong* is a multiplatform video game based on the hit film.

King Kong has inspired all sorts of other things as well. The big ape and the movie about him have sparked everything from a well-known South African musical to songs by rockers the Kinks and Frank Zappa. A professional wrestler in the 1980s called himself King Kong. And in 2005, New Zealand issued a stamp set honoring the release of the film by that nation's most famous director.

Clearly, King Kong is here to stay. He will no doubt continue to command audiences—on the big screen and in movie fans' imaginations—for many years to come. Kong rules!

Notes

Chapter One: The Biggest Gorilla

1. Quoted in Ronald Gottesman and Harry Geduld, eds., *The Girl in the Hairy Paw: King Kong as Myth, Movie, and Monster.* New York: Avon, 1976, p. 19.

Chapter Two: The Original Kong

2. Quoted in Ray Morton, *King Kong: The History of a Movie Icon from Fay Wray to Peter Jackson.* New York: Applause, 2005, p. 8.
3. Quoted in Gene Wright, *Who's Who and What's What in Science Fiction: Film, Television, Radio, and Theater.* New York: Bonanza, 1983, p. 218.
4. Quoted in Morton, *King Kong,* p. 78.

Chapter Three: The Return of Kong

5. Quoted in Morton, *King Kong,* p. 317.
6. Quoted in Jenny Wake, *The Making of* King Kong: *The Official Guide to the Motion Picture.* New York: Pocket Books, 2005, p. 145.

Chapter Four: Kong in the World

7. Quoted in Internet Movie Database, "Memorable Quotes from Jurassic Park." www.imdb.com/title/tt0107290/quotes/.

GLOSSARY

biplanes: The two-winged airplanes commonly used in the 1920s and 1930s.

box office: The amount of money earned by a movie in theaters.

breadlines: Lines in which poor and homeless people stand to receive free food.

cameo: A brief appearance in a movie, often by a well-known person.

collectibles: Rare or unusual items that are sometimes valuable.

documentaries: Nonfiction movies about real-life subjects.

evolution: The process by which animal species can change slowly over many years and generations.

frame: A single photo that is part of movie film.

memorabilia: Items that are connected with special events, people, or things.

sacrificing: The giving up of something valuable, often for the good of a group as a whole.

screenplay: The written script of a film.

stole: A fur piece that wraps around the shoulders.

trilogy: A group of three stories or films, as in the three *Lord of the Rings* movies.

43

FOR FURTHER EXPLORATION

BOOKS

Orville Goldner and George E. Turner, *The Making of King Kong: The Story Behind a Film Classic.* South Brunswick, NJ: A. S. Barnes, 1975. Though not written for children, this detailed book is full of photos about the making of the original film.

Ray Morton, *King Kong: The History of a Movie Icon from Fay Wray to Peter Jackson.* New York: Applause, 2005. This book was not written for children, but it has many wonderful photos. It focuses on the original 1933 movie and the 1976 remake, with only a small section on the 2005 version.

Ian Thorne, *King Kong.* Mankato, MN: Crestwood House, 1977. This simple book follows the stories of the first *King Kong,* its sequel, *Son of Kong,* and other early Kong movies, with photos.

Jenny Wake, *The Making of* King Kong: *The Official Guide to the Motion Picture.* New York: Pocket Books, 2005. Written for older kids, this book is full of terrific photos and other graphic information.

WEB SITES

KongisKing.net–King Kong Movie News and Rumors (www.kongisking.net). An extensive site that archives all of Peter Jackson's production diaries and has much more about the 2005 *King Kong* and other productions.

The Greatest Films, *King Kong* **(1933)** (www.film-site.net/kingk.net). This site is maintained by film scholar Tim Dirks. It has a lot of information about the original film, along with reproductions of posters.

King Kong (www.kingkong.com) The official site of the 2005 version of the movie, this has a wealth of material, such as a section detailing the movie's imaginary creatures.

Peter Jackson's King Kong–The Official Game of the Movie (www.kingkonggame.com). This site describes the video game released in connection with the 2005 movie.

A Boyd Company, King Kong–The Eighth Wonder of the World! (www.aboyd.com/kong/index2.html). Though it needs updates about the latest developments, this site, maintained by film scholar Boyd Campbell, has excellent trivia and information about the 1933 version and many of its spinoffs.

INDEX

Picture Credits

Cover: Universal/Wing Nut Films/Kobal Collection
Dreamworks/Aardman Animation/The Kobal Collection, 35
Getty Images, 40
Hulton Archive/Getty Images, 14, 18, 39
New Line/Saul Zaentz/Wing Nut/The Kobal Collection, 24
Photofest, 5, 6, 11
RKO/Kobal Collection, 16, 19, 21
© Swim Ink 2, LLC/CORBIS, 37
Toho/The Kobal Collection, 33
Universal/Wing Nut Films/Kobal Collection, 8, 9, 26, 27, 29, 31

About the Author

Adam Woog has written more than fifty books for adults, young adults, and children. He lives in Seattle, Washington, with his wife and daughter. They sometimes watch Seattle TV stations KING and KONG.